Proverbios y dichos Mexicanos

FOLK WISDOM of MEXICO

Jeff M. Sellers
Foreword by Gary Soto

Illustrations by
Annika Maria Nelson

CHRONICLE BOOKS
SAN FRANCISCO

Printed in Hong Kong.

Library of Congress Cataloging-in-Publication Data:
Folk wisdom of Mexico = Proverbios y
   dichos mexicanos / [compiled] by Jeff M.
   Sellers ; foreword by Gary Soto ;
   illustrations by Annika Maria Nelson.
       p.   cm.
    ISBN 0-8118-0513-1 (hc)
     1. Proverbs, Mexican. I. Sellers, Jeff M.
    II. Title: Proverbios y dichos mexicanos.
    PN6495.M4F65   1994
    398.9'61'0972—dc20   93-30338
                                          CIP

Translation advisors: Michael Bradburn-Ruster
   and Myrna Villa
Book and cover design: Karen Pike
Composition: TBH/Typecast, Inc.
Cover illustration: Annika Maria Nelson

Distributed in Canada by Raincoast Books,
8680 Cambie Street, Vancouver, B.C. V6P 6M9

10 9 8 7 6 5 4

Chronicle Books
85 Second Street
San Francisco, CA 94105

Web Site: www.chroniclebooks.com

FOREWORD

Several years ago I was invited to give a presentation of my writings for young people at an elementary school in the San Joaquin Valley. I knew that most of the students would be Mexican or Mexican-American, and I had the hunch that they might like to view my collection of Mexican crafts. I was right on this account. I displayed my carved wooden animals, my clay bells, a few articles of embroidered clothing from Oaxaca, some clay and tin whistles, a tray of *milagros,* my *sarape* woven by Zacarias Ruiz of Teotitlán del Valle, and just about everything in my household that sparkled and was imbued with cultural beauty. I even displayed a pair of *aretes* — earrings — on a white cloth. The children enjoyed them, turning them over in their hands. Luckily for me, not one broke.

In one class period I brought out a typed and photocopied list of proverbs and riddles. My intention was to keep the children guessing and wondering with curiosity at things that are Mexican. The proverbs and riddles were in Spanish with English translations. So I stood up in front of the class with the answers in my hands, asking, "OK, who can answer why the egg went blind?" I imagined that I would baffle and tease them, but I was wrong. Hands shot up like a tribe of spears and pained looks saying "Call on me! Call on me!" squinched up their faces. I was the one who was baffled. The book from which I had drawn the riddles was an obscure text from the Chicano Studies library at U.C. Berkeley, certainly not readily accessible to the public, let alone these children who lived far from Berkeley. How could these *esquincles* know that it was the farmer who had poked the eyes out of his two eggs at breakfast? Right then I understood who these kids were: rural children from Mexican families who had been hearing a litany of proverbs since birth. The game was quickly over for me. Suddenly the tables were turned: these fourth-graders were asking me if I could answer some proverbs and riddles that they knew. I was terrifically embarrassed because I couldn't answer even one in my *pocho* Spanish. Surely, I thought, there must be a proverb about the bigshot teacher who is taught a good lesson by students with grass stains on their knees!

The Mexican proverb is the verbal property of common people. It is a condensed saying, some pithy remark from a man leaning on his plow or a woman with her elbows up on a table as she listens to the *chisme* — gossip — of a neighbor. The Mexican proverb may inform and advise, or it may offer an arguable point to life. It is amusement and it is wisdom itself. It is the snappy scolding of a naughty child. It is the soothing remedy to loss and the loss of hope. It is the logic of unrequited love and the finger-wagging judgment on greed and gluttony. It is warning and conclusion. It is the unwritten literature and philosophy of the poor, particularly rural folk. While the wealthy and educated have Carlos Fuentes and Octavio Paz, the man or woman on the street has songs, limericks, folklore, *chisme,* and proverbs such as *"Quien más mira menos ve"* (The more one looks, the less one sees). So much for focused and mind-tiring education, this proverb seems to conclude.

Most Mexican proverbs have been passed down from generation to generation with only a sign of changes. They are frequently regional yet universal in appeal. That they have European roots is certain, and that they have been shared verbally instead of in books is also certain. Mexican proverbs may not be as old as rock, but they are at least as old as the largest trees in the *zocalos* of rural towns. They share the qualities of proverbs from other cultures: they are sharp and distilled truths.

Proverbs reunite the listener with his or her ancestors. They bear witness to the ancient human foibles that continue to plague us to this day. It takes only a kitchen table, or two chairs situated under a mulberry tree, to hear a chattering of rural history summed up with an appropriate proverb. If you are like me, the grandson of *una abuela* who came to the United States at the end of the Mexican revolution, you might hear a story from a seventy-two-year-old woman, who heard it from her grandmother Graciela Trevino, who heard it first from her *tía,* the aunt who was widowed for no more than two years before taking up with that rake Don José López, who was a good man in the end and, *pues,* responsible for digging a well in San Pedro Piedra Gorda, Zacatecas—or so the history might have it between sips of coffee. In turn, proverbs as well as tales live through the passing of a day and not in the turning of a page.

The farther north Mexicans have trudged into the United States, the fewer proverbs one hears in conversation. There may be fewer occasions to use them in these new surroundings or fewer people to appreciate the clever language. They begin to disappear within one generation, along with the use of Spanish, and are replaced with less clever phrasings. Children perk up more to television jingles and words from pop songs than they do to proverbs, Mexican or otherwise. They know the faces of rock stars and celebrities. They know athletes and brand names. In short, the world for them is so visual that their verbal dexterity is limited to the momentary zing of commercials and advertisements.

Folk Wisdom of Mexico is a gathering of proverbs that will delight and awaken us with their brilliance.

They are more honest, accurate, and wise than any one of us because they have traveled through the soothing whisperings of years. They can be relished, memorized, quoted in Spanish and English, tested on friends, and finally evaluated in one's own life. They are meant to put us in our place and then console us as we feel the weight of mortality, we, this *generación de mocosos* who seldom listened to our elders. Now we live up to the proverb *"El muchacho malcriado dondequiera encuentra padre."* For the meaning of this in English, you'll have to look in these pages.

Gary Soto

Introduction

The same curious mixture of fatalism and faith and laughter and death that surfaces in Mexican folk culture makes for some pithy proverbs. Out of such mixes come spicy ironies that have formed into little twists of wisdom, all peculiar to that nation. As they say regarding the unique, "Like Mexico, there is but one."

In fact, they say, "Like Mexico, there aren't two," but I feel that that does not sound or feel as gallant and proud as the original Spanish saying, *"Como México, no hay dos."* The literal translation loses all rhythm. So it is that some liberties must be taken in the translation of these proverbs. My intent was to give them a sound and feel similar to the Spanish originals, while remaining as true as possible to their literal meanings, ideas, and words.

Where the same sound or feel could not be duplicated in English, I sought rhythms and rhymes that evoke the Spanish. The charm of the proverbs themselves does the rest.

It is true that most Mexican proverbs have their roots in Spain. The scholars I consulted—except for those who compile the profane street sayings of modern Mexico, which I chose not to include—trace most of the proverbs to sayings originally popular in Spain.

All of those proverbs, however, have evolved into distinctly Mexican species. The voice of the proverbs in *Folk Wisdom of Mexico* is uniquely Mexican and completely fresh. If, as the proverb says, "Conversation is food for the soul," then settle in and let this book speak to you.

Proverbios y dichos Mexicanos

FOLK WISDOM of MEXICO

En boca cerrada no entran moscas.
Flies don't enter a closed mouth.

15

*No es lo mismo hablar de toros que estar en
el redondel.*

Talking about bulls is not the same as facing them
in the ring.

Al mal músico hasta las uñas le estorban.

Even fingernails get in the way of a bad musician.

*Dios les da el dinero a los ricos, porque si no lo
tuvieran, se morirían de hambre.*

God gives money to the wealthy because without it,
they would starve to death.

*Mal comienza la semana aquel que es ahorcado
en lunes.*

It's a bad start on the week for the man who is
hanged on a Monday.

*El que ansioso escoge lo mejor suele quedarse con
lo peor.*

He who is anxious to secure the best tends to get
stuck with the worst of the rest.

Al nopal lo van a ver sólo cuando tiene tunas.
The prickly pear has company only when it
bears fruit.

El valiente vive hasta que el cobarde quiere.
The brave one lives as long as the coward lets him.

*No hay mal que dure cien años, ni enfermo que
los resista.*
No pain lasts 100 years, nor could anyone
outlast them.

Como dijo la mosca, "¡Andamos arando!"
The fly atop the ox declares: "We are plowing this field!"

Para tonto no se estudia.
One needn't study to become a fool.

Hay más tiempo que vida.
There is more time than life.

Cuando menos burros, más olotes.
The fewer the donkeys, the more ears of corn.

El que nunca va a tu casa en la suya no te quiere.

He who never goes to your house doesn't want you in his.

Hay que aprender a perder antes de saber jugar.

One must learn how to lose before learning how to play.

El que parte y comparte, se queda con la mejor parte.

He who divides and shares is left with the best share.

Guarda tu ayuda para quien te la pida.
Keep your counsel arrested until it's requested.

La amistad sincera es un alma repartida en dos cuerpos.

True friendship is one soul shared by two bodies.

No hagas hoy lo que puedas hacer mañana.
Don't do today what you can put off until
tomorrow.

El mejor caballo necesita espuelas.
Even the best horse needs to be spurred.

Anda tu camino sin ayuda de vecino.
Walk your own road and bear your own load.

La conversación es el pasto del alma.
Conversation is food for the soul.

La verdad padece pero no perece.
Truth suffers but never perishes.

Con paciencia y salivita un elefante se coge a una hormiguita.
With patience and a bit of spittle the elephant picks up the ant so little.

*No hay que andarse por las ramas estando tan
grueso el tronco.*

There's no reason to walk on the branches when
the trunk is so thick.

Más vale morir parado que vivir de rodillas.
Better to die on your feet than to live on
your knees.

Cuando en duda, consúltalo con tu almohada.
When in doubt of what is right, consult your
pillow overnight.

*A la hora de freir frijoles, lo que hace falta es
la manteca.*
When it's time to fry the beans, you can't do
without lard.

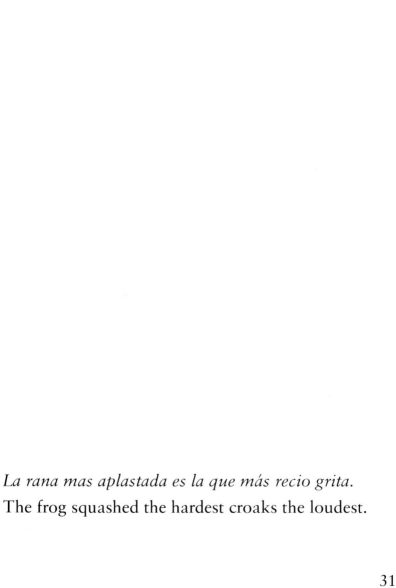

La rana mas aplastada es la que más recio grita.
The frog squashed the hardest croaks the loudest.

También de dolor se canta cuando llorar no se puede.

Sorrow also sings, when it runs too deep to cry.

*No hay vida más cansada que el eterno no hacer
nada.*
There's no life as tiring as one always retiring.

El que mucho abarca, poco aprieta.
He who grabs much grasps little.

Del árbol caído todos hacen leña.
From the fallen tree everyone makes firewood.

La necedad cierra las puertas de la bondad.
Stupidity closes the doors of kindness.

*Más vale burro que arrear que no carga
que cargar.*
Better a donkey that tarries than one that won't
carry its load.

*Más vale gotita permanente que aguacero
de repente.*
Better a steady drip than a sudden deluge.

En cuestión de puercos todo es dinero, y en cuestión de dinero todos son puercos.

In the matter of pigs, all is money, and in the matter of money, all are pigs.

Más hace una hormiga andando que un buey echado.

An ant on the move does more than a dozing ox.

37

Mientras dura, vida y dulzura.
While life yet lasts, laughter and molasses.

*No hay corazón tan triste como una bolsa
sin dinero.*
There's no heart as sad as an empty purse.

Desconfía de tu mejor amigo como de tu peor enemigo.

Trust your best friend as you would your worst enemy.

El que da primero da dos veces.

He who strikes first strikes twice.

No da el que puede, sino el que quiere.

It's not the able that give, but the desirous.

El muerto a la sepulrura, y el vivo a la travesura.
The dead to his burial ground, and the living to his fooling around.

41

Dios habla por el que calla.
God speaks for the man who holds his peace.

La ambición nunca se llena.
Ambition never has its fill.

Una onza de alegría vale más que una onza de oro.
An ounce of gladness is worth more than an ounce of gold.

Costal vacío no se para.
An empty bag will not stay up.

La sangre sin fuego hierve.
Blood boils without flame.

El que quiera azul celeste, que le cueste.
For whoever wants the blue sky, the price is high.

Contestación sin pregunta, señal de culpa.
An answer without a question signals guilt without question.

No hay mejor salsa que un buen apetito.
There's no better sauce than a good appetite.

No hay camino más seguro que el que acaban de robar.

No road is safer than the one just robbed.

Sólo lo barato se compra con el dinero.

Money buys only what is cheap.

Más vale una vez colorado que ciento descolorido.

Better to be red-faced once than 100 times purple.

Cada quien puede hacer de sus calzones
un papalote.
Every man is entitled to make a kite from his pants.

Ganar un pleito es adquirir un pollo y perder una vaca.

To win a dispute is to gain a chicken and lose a cow.

Alabanza en boca propia es vituperio.
Self-praise amounts to self-condemnation.

El que no llora no mama.
He who doesn't fuss isn't nursed.

Mata más una esperanza que un desengaño.
False hope kills more readily than bitter truth.

De veneno, basta una sola gota.
With poison, one drop is enough.

*Al gusto y a la tristeza, no hay que darles
rienda suelta.*
In pleasure or in pain, give neither free rein.

Cada quien tiene su forma de matar a pulgas.
Everyone has their own way of killing fleas.

No le tengan miedo al chile aunque lo
vean colorado.

Don't be afraid of the chile pepper, even though
it's so red.

No la chifles que es cantada.
Don't whistle what should be sung.

*El que mucho mal padece con poco bien
se conforma.*
He who suffers many evils is comforted with just
a little good.

El que es buen pato hasta en el aire nada.
A good duck can swim even in the air.

*Todo el rato que está enojado, pierde de
estar contento.*

All time spent angry is time lost being happy.

*Las deudas viejas no se pagan, y las nuevas se
dejan envejecer.*

Old debts are not paid, and new ones are left to
get old.

El que es perico, dondequiera es verde.
He who is a parrot is green wherever he is.

El que temprano se moja tiempo tiene de secarse.
He who gets drenched at dawn has the rest of the day to dry out.

Es mejor estar solo que mal acompañado.
Better alone unattached than unsuitably matched.

El que con lobos anda a aullar se enseña.
He who walks with wolves learns to howl.

Más vale paso que dure y no trote que canse.
Better a stride that will last than a trot that
tires fast.

La malicia va más allá de la realidad.
Malice leaves reality behind.

*Sólo el que carga el cajón sabe lo que pesa
el muerto.*

Only the pallbearers know the weight of the dead.

Cada quien es dueño de su miedo.
Everyone is master of their own fear.

Aunque la jaula sea de oro, no deja de ser prisión.
Though the cage be made of gold, it's still a prison.

Todos dicen que maten al toro, pero el toro no mate a nadie.

The whole arena tells them to kill the bull, yet the bull should kill no one.

Qué bonito es ver llover y no mojarse.
How beautiful to watch the rain and not get wet.

Cuando joven, de ilusiones; cuando viejo,
de recuerdos.
While young, it's all dreams; when old,
all memories.

El sueño es alimento de los pobres.
Dreaming is the food of the poor.

Arriba ya del caballo, hay que aguantar los respingos.
Once mounted on a horse, one must hang on when he bucks.

Ojos que no ven, tienen menos que sentir.
Eyes that don't see have less to lament.

Sobre gustos no hay nada escrito.
As to tastes, nothing is written.

No hay peor lucha que la que no se hace.
There's no worse struggle than one that
never begins.

Querer es poder.
Where there's a will there's a way.

Llórate pobre, y no te llores sólo.
Bewail your poverty, and not alone.

El carnicero de hoy es la res de mañana.
Today's butcher is tomorrow's beef.

No hagas cosas buenas que parezcan malas.
Don't do good that could look bad.

Más vale ser perro de rico que santo de pobre.
Better to be a rich man's dog than a poor
man's saint.

65

El muchacho malcriado dondequiera encuentra padre.

The ill-mannered child finds a father wherever he goes.

Tanto peca el que mata la vaca como el que le tiene la pata.

He who holds the heifer for the slaughter is as much a killer as the slayer.

Quien con la esperanza vive, alegre muere.
He who lives with hope dies happy.

Mar tranquilo hace mal marino.
Calm seas make sorry sailors.

*Si quieres tu lumbre apagar, echa tortillas
a calentar.*
If you want your campfire under control, throw
some tortillas on the coal.

El que demonios da, diablos recibe.
He who gives demons receives devils.

Músico pagado toca mal son.
A paid musician plays a poor tune.

*A todo se acostumbra el hombre, menos a
no comer.*
Man can adjust to anything except not eating.

De médico, poeta, músico y loco todos tenemos un poco.

Of doctor and poet, musician and madman we each have a trace.

Un hombre sin alegría no es bueno o no está bueno.

A man without happiness is either not good or not well.

La esperanza muere al último.
Hope dies last of all.

El mejor torero es el de la barrera.
The best bullfighter is the one in the box seats.

Haz el bien y no veas a quien.
Do good and don't worry to whom.

Al buen entendedor, pocas palabras.
To those apt to understand, few words.

El flojo trabaja doble.
The lazy work twice as much.

Quien más mira menos ve.
The more one looks, the less one sees.

Hay veces que nada el pato, y hay otras que ni agua bebe.

There are times when the duck swims in the water, and others when he won't even drink it.

Todo por servir se acaba.

Everything wears away from use.

Vale más un grito a tiempo que hablar a cada momento.

Better one timely squawk than constant talk.

El delito acusa.
The crime itself accuses.

Quien todo lo quiere todo lo pierde.
He who wants everything will lose everything.

El tiempo cura y nos mata.
Time heals and then it kills.

El sol es la cobija del pobre.
The sun is the blanket of the poor.